Nobody!

A Story About Overcoming Bullying in Schools

by Erin Frankel

illustrated by Paula Heaphy

free spirit
PUBLISHING®

Acknowledgments

Heartfelt thanks to our dedicated and talented team at Free Spirit Publishing including Judy Galbraith, Meg Bratsch, Alison Behnke, Steven Hauge, Michelle Lee Lagerroos, Margie Lisovskis, and Anastasia Scott. Special gratitude to all of our friends and family whose creative inspiration and encouragement made this book possible, including Gabriela, Sofia, and Kelsey Cadahia; Ludwig Bryngelsson; Thomas and William Ruse; Sam Perrottet; Mackenzie Marsden; Ian Phares; Thomas Heaphy; Beth Rusc; Naomi Drew; Beth Moriarty; and Alvaro Cadahia. In loving memory of Gillian Donnelly—whose kindness lives on forever.

Library of Congress Cataloging-in-Publication Data
Frankel, Erin, author.
Nobody! : a story about overcoming bullying in schools / by Erin Frankel; illustrated by Paula Heaphy.
       pages cm
  Summary: In school Kyle's persistent bullying is making Thomas feel like a nobody, and he needs help from his classmates and adults to understand and recapture his self-esteem—but Kyle needs help too. Includes activities for children and information on recognizing and preventing bullying for adults.
  ISBN 978-1-57542-496-5 (soft cover) — ISBN 978-1-57542-495-8 (hard cover)
 1. Bullying in schools—Juvenile fiction. 2. Self-esteem—Juvenile fiction. [1. Bullying—Fiction. 2. Self-esteem—Fiction. 3. Schools—Fiction.] I. Heaphy, Paula, illustrator. II. Title.
  PZ7.1.F75No 2015
  [E]—dc23
                                                                    2014034684

Reading Level Grade 2; Interest Level Ages 5–9;
Fountas & Pinnell Guided Reading Level M

Edited by Meg Bratsch and Alison Behnke
Cover and interior design by Michelle Lee Lagerroos
Photo of Erin Frankel by Gabriela Cadahia; photo of Paula Heaphy by Travis Huggett
Bugs on page 41 © Zobeedy | Dreamstime.com

10 9 8 7 6 5 4 3 2 1
Printed in Hong Kong
P17200215

Free Spirit Publishing Inc.
Minneapolis, MN
(612) 338-2068
help4kids@freespirit.com
www.freespirit.com

FSC
www.fsc.org
MIX
Paper from
responsible sources
FSC® C018769

Free Spirit offers competitive pricing.
Contact edsales@freespirit.com for pricing information on multiple quantity purchases.

To everybody who has
ever made a difference in
somebody's story.

You matter.

Nobody is more important
than you.

I used to like school. But that was before somebody decided to make my life miserable.

Before somebody named Kyle
made me feel like a NOBODY!

I thought things would be better this year now that Kyle isn't in my class, but I was wrong.

Now he just finds new places and ways to mess with me.

Mom said Kyle would grow up over the summer and stop picking on me, but he didn't grow up. He just grew.

I thought I'd get a break from Kyle at soccer practice. But guess who's on my team this year?

Doesn't he have anything better to do than make fun of me? I know **I** have better things to do.

Problem is, I can't get him off my mind sometimes.

I don't even enjoy the things I'm good at anymore.

Everyone tells me, "Just stay away from him."
But why doesn't **he** stay away from **me?**
It's not like I'm the one following him around.

I tell him to stop, but he doesn't listen.
At least not when **I** say it.

When I try telling someone what Kyle's doing, he always says the same thing: "I didn't do anything!" And if nobody else speaks up, then it's my word against his.

I wish some people would look a little closer when Kyle is mean to me.

I'm getting tired of the same old story.
Kyle acts mean, I feel bad.

Or even worse . . .
Kyle acts mean to me,
and I act mean to somebody else.

But no one wants to make him mad.

If I were him, I'd think again.

Still . . . what if Kyle is right?
What if nobody is like me?

What if I **am** different?

20

But aren't we all different in some way?

Isn't that what makes things interesting?

What if I try
looking at things
differently?

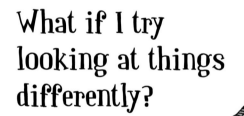

I've decided it's time for a new story.

I wish it could go something like this . . .

But when the moment comes, I get stuck.

Which is why it feels really good
when other people speak up with me!

And that it's okay
to need a little help
with his feelings
sometimes . . .

just like the
rest of us.

Lately, Kyle seems to be acting a little better.

32

He's starting to think twice
about what to say and do.

I've been thinking twice about things, too.

I've decided that **nobody** can make me feel like a nobody.

And there's nothing wrong with being me, 'cause I really am . . .

Thomas says . . .

When I was being bullied, I felt like a nobody. Here are some of the things that helped me get back to being the somebody I wanted to be:

- I started to believe that I'm somebody important—because I am! When you believe in yourself, nobody can make you feel like a nobody.

- I decided not to give up the things I enjoy just because of something somebody says or does.

- I chose friends who like me for who I am.

- I tried looking at things differently. Our differences make us interesting!

Jay says . . .

When Thomas was being bullied, I tried to be a good friend so he wouldn't feel alone. Here are some of the things that made a difference:

- I showed that I cared about Thomas by hanging out with him and doing stuff we both enjoyed.

- I let Thomas know that people (like me!) think he's great just the way he is.

- I helped Thomas avoid Kyle when he wanted to.

- I told my other friends that we could help Thomas look at things differently.

Patrick says . . .

Even though Thomas and I weren't close friends, I felt bad about the way Kyle was treating him, and I wanted to do something to make it stop. Here are some of the ways I stood up for Thomas:

- I didn't laugh when Kyle was acting mean to Thomas. When I felt safe, I told Kyle to stop.

- I let Kyle see me hanging out with Thomas. Hanging out with nice people is cool. It isn't something to hide.

- I told Mr. C when I saw Kyle and his friends being mean to Thomas. If Mr. C hadn't been around, I would have told another adult I trusted.

- When Kyle pushed me on the soccer field, I stood up for myself. That helps other kids see that they can do it, too.

> ## *Telling vs. Tattling
> Nobody wants to be a tattletale. But tattling on a person for doing something small (like cutting in line) is *very different* from telling an adult when someone needs help. If you were being bullied, you'd want someone to help you, right?

Kyle says . . .

I got in the bad habit of saying and doing mean things to Thomas without even thinking about how it would make him feel. Here are some of the tips I learned on how to start being kind to somebody:

- I started to stop and think before I said or did something. Taking my time helps me choose to be kind.

- I imagined how Thomas would feel if I did or said something mean. I also thought about how I would feel.

- I paid attention to how other people reacted when I was mean to Thomas. Nobody seemed to like it. When I stopped acting mean and started acting nice, I noticed that everyone was friendlier with me.

- I tried saying something positive to somebody every day. It felt good, so I kept practicing. Before long, being kind was a new habit!

Sign Up for Thomas's Team Somebody

When Kyle was bullying me, I just wanted to be somebody different—somebody Kyle *didn't* pick on. But I had a team of people cheering me on and that made me feel really good. I'm glad that Kyle had people cheering him on, too. Thanks to everyone working together as a team, Kyle realized that he could be somebody who *doesn't* pick on others.

Team Somebody is always looking for new players. Hey, what about you? Come and join the fun! You can make a difference, too. Try these ideas to get started.

Nice Play!

I'm glad that Kyle is trying out a new play. He's thinking twice about what he says and does, and that's a big win! With everyone acting better, our team is scoring more points than ever. And we're having more fun off the field, too. Coach says that some plays will only lead us out of bounds. If it isn't a nice play, then it's better not to take it.

Ready for practice? Find the nice plays below that will lead you toward a goal. Now find the ones that will lead you out of bounds. How many of each did you see? Remember, nice plays score big!

"Want to play with us?"

"Nice pass."

"Good game!"

"I don't want you on my team."

"Crybaby!"

"Are you okay?"

"Need a hand?"

"I've got your back."

"Loser!"

"What's your problem?"

"You made us lose!"

Look at It Differently

When Kyle put me down, I put myself down, too. I kept thinking I was just no good. But I realized that negative thoughts are like stinging bugs. Every time you think or say a negative thought, it hurts. So I tried looking at things in a positive way. When I decided to change my story from *No*body to *Some*body, I started to feel more confident, and that made it easier to stand up for myself. I realized that we're all different—and that's okay. It's what makes life interesting!

You can look at things differently, too. Find an old jar and some paper. Cut the paper into shapes of things you like.

Next, write down some negative and positive thoughts on the cutouts. Put them in the jar, and shake them all up. Take them out one at a time. If you get a positive thought, put it back in the jar. If it's a negative thought, try to think of a different way to look at it. On a new cutout, write a positive thought that turns that negative idea around. Then crumple up those stinging negative thoughts and throw them away. When you only have positive thoughts left, decorate your jar and keep it handy. Whenever you need help looking at things differently, reach in and grab a reminder.

Find Somebody

I found out that it's okay to need help with our feelings. Lots of important people helped me see that my feelings matter. And Kyle had people who helped him, too. Now I know that I get to choose my own story—and I can also decide to be somebody important in someone else's story. We all can! Join Team Somebody and find someone like the people who helped me change my story from Nobody to Somebody. See if you can find somebody who is:

kind   honest   understanding
     helpful   brave   caring

Now, draw a picture or write a sentence about why you picked that person. (Or, if you're reading with somebody, have a chat about it.) Can you think of people in your life who helped when you were having a hard time? And how about you? What kind of "somebody" do you want to be for others?

A Note to Parents, Teachers, and Other Caring Adults

Why can't everybody just be kind to each other? Why is it so difficult to get along? These are the questions we ask ourselves when we hear stories of bullying. But for those who experience the pain of bullying firsthand, questions often turn into self-doubt. Like Thomas in *Nobody!*, children who are targets of bullying may wonder if their differences are the reason they are being bullied. As caring adults, we can help children understand that our differences are causes for celebration—and that they are never justification for mean behavior. At the same time, for children who find it difficult to get along with others, we can offer compassion and guidance to help them develop the skills to make kinder choices. We can watch for opportunities to help children feel supported, and empower upstanders like Jay and Patrick to support others. And through stories such as *Nobody!*, we can help children grow in empathy so that they will be able to look beyond differences and see what we all share in common: The desire and need for love, kindness, and respect.

Reflection Questions for *Nobody!*

The story told in *Nobody!* is a fictional situation, but it is one that many kids will likely relate to, even if their exact experiences have been different. Use these questions to encourage reflection and dialogue as you read *Nobody!* Referring to characters by name will help children make connections: *Thomas* is the target of the bullying; *Jay* and *Patrick* are bystanders to the bullying; and *Kyle* initiates the bullying.

Page 1: Why do you think Thomas wants to stay home from school?

Pages 2–5: How do you think Thomas feels when Kyle says something mean to him? What are the other characters doing? Why do you think some people laugh along when someone is acting mean?

Pages 6–12: How do people around Thomas help—or not help—when Kyle is being mean?

Think about Jay, Patrick, Mr. C., and others. Why does Thomas wish that some people would look a little closer when Kyle bullies him? How does Thomas feel when his sister sees him being bullied at the bus stop? Have you ever felt this way? Why do you think it's hard for Thomas to stop thinking about Kyle?

Page 13: Why do you think it is difficult for Thomas to talk about bullying? Why do you think Thomas yells at his mom?

Pages 14–17: How do you think other kids feel when they are around Kyle? What about adults? Why do you think Thomas's mom is worried about Kyle?

Pages 18–19: Why did Patrick tell Mr. C. about what was happening to Thomas? Why don't Kyle's friends tell Mr. C. that they were laughing along when Kyle was being mean? How do you think Kyle feels about what his friends say?

Pages 20–23: What helps Thomas think about himself differently? How does being different make something or someone interesting?

Pages 24–27: Why is it hard to stand up for ourselves when someone says or does something mean? How do Thomas's friends help make it easier for him to stand up for himself? Have you ever stood up for someone? How did that person feel? How did you feel?

Pages 28–29: What happens now when Kyle says or does something mean? How is it different from the beginning of the story? *Why* is it different?

Pages 30–31: How do caring adults help Kyle and Thomas? Who are adults you can talk to about your feelings?

Pages 32–33: What does Kyle do or say to show that he is working to be kinder? How do you think Thomas feels about Kyle now?

Pages 34–37: Why does Thomas change the title of his story from Nobody to Somebody? What has Thomas discovered about himself?

Overall: Which character in *Nobody!* is most like you and why? What would you like to say to this character?

> *Important:* **Online bullying (called *cyberbullying*) is a real concern among elementary-age children, given the increased use of smartphones and computers in school and at home. It's also the most difficult type of bullying to stop, because it's less apparent to onlookers. Be sure to include cyberbullying in all of your discussions about bullying with kids.**

About the Author and Illustrator

Erin Frankel has a master's degree in English education and is passionate about parenting, teaching, and writing. Erin knows firsthand what it feels like to be bullied, and she hopes her stories will help children stay true to who they are and help put an end to bullying. She and longtime friend Paula Heaphy are grateful to be able to spread a message of kindness through their books. In her free time, Erin loves chasing after her doggie Bella in the woods of Pittsburgh and traveling to Spain with her husband Alvaro and their three daughters, Gabriela, Sofia, and Kelsey.

Paula Heaphy is a textile designer in the fashion industry. She's an explorer of all artistic mediums from glassblowing to shoemaking, but her biggest love is drawing. She jumped at the chance to illustrate her friend Erin's stories, having been bullied herself as a child. Together, they envisioned the Weird series: *Weird!*, *Dare!*, and *Tough!*, a story of bullying told from three perspectives. Paula lives in Brooklyn, New York, where she hopes to use her creativity to light up the hearts of children for years to come.

Interested in purchasing multiple quantities and receiving volume discounts?
Contact edsales@freespirit.com or call 1.800.735.7323 and ask for Education Sales.

Many Free Spirit authors are available for speaking engagements, workshops, and keynotes.
Contact speakers@freespirit.com or call 1.800.735.7323.

For pricing information, to place an order, or to request a free catalog, contact:

free spirit PUBLISHING®

**217 Fifth Avenue North • Suite 200 • Minneapolis, MN 55401-1299 • toll-free 800.735.7323 • local 612.338.2068
fax 612.337.5050 • help4kids@freespirit.com • www.freespirit.com**